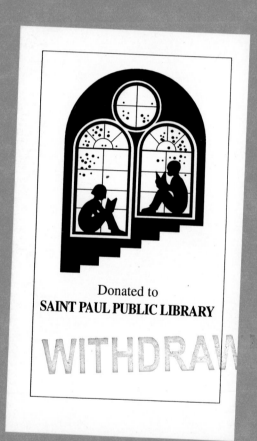

# MAKE it WORK!

# EARTH

## Wendy Baker & Andrew Haslam

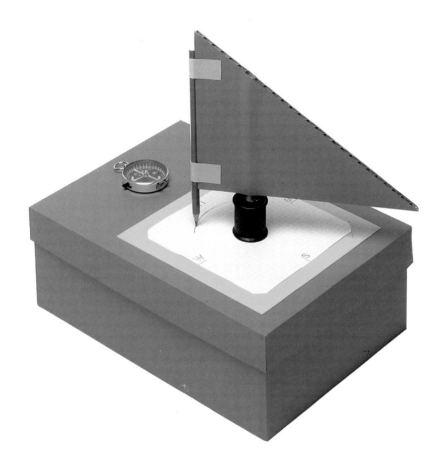

*written by*
*Alexandra Parsons*

*photography by*
*Jon Barnes*

A **TWO-CAN** BOOK
published by
**THOMSON LEARNING**
New York

## MAKE it WORK!
## Other titles

Body
Building
Electricity
Flight
Insects
Machines
Plants
Sound
Universe

This edition published in the United States in 1995 by
Thomson Learning, New York

First published in Great Britain in 1992 by
Two-Can Publishing Ltd.

**Library of Congress Cataloging-in-Publication Data**

Parsons, Alexandra.
  Earth / Alexandra Parsons. – – 1st Thomson Learning ed.
    p.    cm.  – – (Make it work!)
  Previously published: New York : Aladdin Bks., 1993. (Make it work!)
  Includes bibliographical references (p.      –  ) and index.
  ISBN  1-56847-468-7  (hc)
  ISBN  1-56847-504-7  (pb)
  1.  Earth sciences – – Experiments – – Juvenile literature.   [1. Earth
sciences – – Experiments.  2. Experiments. ]  I. Title.  II. Series.
QE29.P385    1995
550'.78 – – dc20                                          95-13992

Printed and bound in Hong Kong

Editor: Mike Hirst
Illustrator: Michael Ogden
Additional design: Belinda Webster

The authors and publishers would like to thank the following for
allowing the reproduction of extracts from their maps in this book:
The Ordnance Survey; Michelin (Map 9, 1992 edn. and Bayern/
Baden-Württemberg Carte Routière et Touristique); Muray, Laurie,
Norie and Wilson Ltd; Bollmann-Bildkarten-Verlag; Instituto Nacional
Para La Conservacion De La Naturaleza; Swiss Federal Office of
Topography (Swiss National Map 1:25,000); Kodansha International
Ltd; Gonsha Travel Publications; National Geographic Society.

Thanks also to: Albert Baker, Catherine Bee, Tony Ellis
and everyone at Plough Studios.

# Contents

Words marked in **bold** in the text are
explained in the glossary.

Have you ever wondered how soil and rocks are formed? How maps are made? Or how television weather forecasters can tell if it will rain or be sunny? Earth scientists know the answers to all of these questions. They study the planet on which we live.

In the study of the earth, many different branches of science overlap. **Geology** investigates the ground under our feet – the planet's soil and rocks. **Meteorology** is the study of the earth's weather. In **geography**, scientists study the earth's surface features – its oceans, mountains, rivers and plains. Start experimenting and become a scientist yourself!

## MAKE it WORK!

By following the projects and experiments in this book, you will be investigating what the earth is made of, how to use maps and how to record and forecast the weather.

## You will need

Most of the activities in this book use simple materials, such as cardboard, glue and old odds and ends. However, you might find a few pieces of specialist equipment useful.

**Geologist's hammer**  This hammer is specially designed for chipping out rock specimens.

**Safety goggles**  These will protect your eyes from flying bits of hard rock. You can buy both goggles and a hammer from a rock and gem dealer, but a small bricklayer's hammer (with a flat head) and goggles from a hardware shop will do the job just as well.

**Pocket magnifier** and **small plastic bags**
These are used for examining and storing rock and soil specimens.

**Notebooks, pens** and **pencils**  You will need these for making notes on all your activities and experiments. Keeping clear records is an important part of a scientist's work.

**Greenhouse thermometer**
Thermometers measure temperature. This special greenhouse thermometer also records highest and lowest temperatures. It is especially useful for keeping track of how hot and cold it is each day.

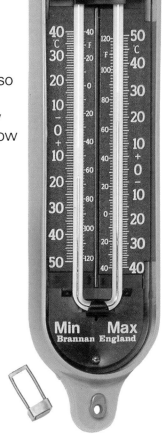

**Camera**  Another good way of recording information is to use a camera. You can take photographs of cloud formations, for instance.

**Compass**  It tells you which direction is north – important for plotting your own maps.

**Maps**  Maps are a way of recording a whole variety of information about the earth. You can buy them in most bookstores, or borrow them from your local library.

*Sometimes nature itself provides us with the special equipment we need for earth-watching experiments. We can even forecast the weather by observing the behavior of plants and animals. Take seaweed, for instance. If you hang a piece outside, it will feel damp when the air is full of moisture and rain is likely. When the air is dry, the seaweed will be too.*

Maps are a good way of recording all sorts of different information about the earth. Some maps give a general picture of the earth's surface features – the hills and valleys, roads and rivers, towns and countries. Other maps contain much more specialized information. There are weather maps and street plans, charts plotting the courses of rivers, and geological maps to show which kinds of rock lie below the soil.

- A **relief map** shows the height and shape of the land, with all its physical features – hills and valleys, rivers and plains.

- **Political maps** show how people have divided up the land, into countries, states and other regions, such as districts and counties.

- A **thematic map** concentrates on giving one particular piece of information. For instance, a thematic map might show varying amounts of rainfall or population levels in different areas.

- An **isometric map** is really a picture that shows an area of land as though you were looking down on it at an angle from the sky.

- **Sea charts** show the depths of seas and oceans, and the shape of the seabed.

Sea chart showing
a harbor

Road map showing
part of Germany

Relief map of a volcano

Relief map of the Alps

Street map of Tokyo

*The oldest map ever to have been discovered by archaeologists was drawn some time around 2,300 B.C. It was made on a small clay tablet and shows an estate in the empire of the ancient Babylonians.*

## MAKE it WORK!

See how many different kinds of maps you can find. You might try to make a collection of your own, but maps can be expensive, so it's probably best to start off by looking in the reference section of your local library. Keep a record of the various maps you find. Study them carefully and then make a list of all the different pieces of information that each map contains.

3-D relief map of
the English Lake District

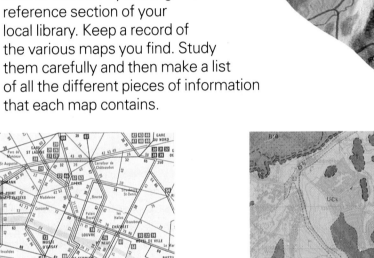

Map showing the lines
of the Paris métro

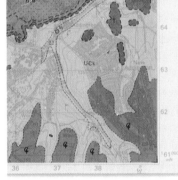

Geological map
showing rock types

Isometric street map
of New York City

Street map of Los Angeles

River chart

The most accurate map of the earth is three-dimensional – a globe. Flat maps can give us a good idea of the shapes of countries and continents, but they are never quite exact. When the curved shapes of the earth are flattened out on paper, they are always distorted, or changed, a little.

**1** Fold a ring of newspaper to make a stand for the soccer ball. Dip strips of old newspaper in the wallpaper paste and cover the ball with three or four smooth layers of papier-mâché. Allow the papier-mâché to dry.

**2** Mix the plaster of Paris with water to make a stiff paste. Smear it onto the globe little by little, molding the shapes of the continents as you go. Keep looking at your map reference to make the shapes as accurate as you can.

## MAKE it WORK!
A good way to find out about the shapes of the earth's continents and oceans is to make your own globe, using an old soccer ball, papier-mâché and cellulose filler.

## You will need
| | |
|---|---|
| an old plastic soccer ball | plaster of Paris |
| old newspapers | a world map |
| wallpaper paste | paints and paintbrushes |

**3** If your map shows mountains and plains, you can try to build up the high areas on the globe and then mold the plains with just a flat, thin layer of filler. Once you've finished molding, allow the globe to dry again.

**4** Paint your globe. Make the oceans blue, the lowlands green, and the mountains brown. Use white paint for the two ice caps at the North and South poles.

Almost 70 percent of the earth's surface is covered by seas and oceans. Only 30 percent is dry land. At the North and South poles, where the rays of the sun are weakest, are the polar ice caps — large areas of land and sea that are covered by snow and ice.

Although we cannot feel it moving, the earth is constantly spinning around, like a top. It makes one complete spin every 24 hours. When part of the earth faces the sun, it has daylight. But as it spins away from the sun, the same area grows dark and moves into nighttime.

**5** Try to find a professional globe and compare it with your own. How accurately have you modeled the shape of the land?

Look again at the maps on pages 6 and 7, and you will see that some of them are crisscrossed by thin black or blue lines. These lines make up the map grid. If you know how the grid works, you can use map reference **coordinates** to pinpoint any spot on the map quickly and exactly.

## MAKE it WORK!

Practice using map coordinates with the treasure island game. First make the boards and pieces. Then follow the rules on pages 12–13 and play the game!

## You will need

colored paper and poster board    glue
pens, pencils, paint, paint brushes    map pins
scissors and X-Acto knife    dice

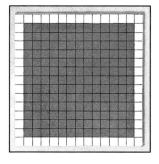 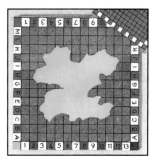

## ▲ Make the main playing board

**1** Take a large piece of poster board, about 30 inches square. Rule grid lines on it, making 15 squares across and 15 down.

**2** Design a treasure island shape and paint it onto the board to show clearly the sea and land areas. Then write the map coordinate letters and numbers around the edge of the board as shown above.

**3** Paint the squares at each corner – one blue, one green, one red and one yellow. These are the starting squares for each player.

## Map coordinates

Map coordinates are usually a combination of a number with a letter – G8, for instance. Finding a coordinate is easy. Each of the grid lines on a map is marked with a letter or a number. (In our game, vertical lines have letters, and horizontal lines have numbers.) To reach G8, you would look for line G along the bottom of the grid, and line 8 up the side. The point G8 is the place on the map where the two grid lines meet.

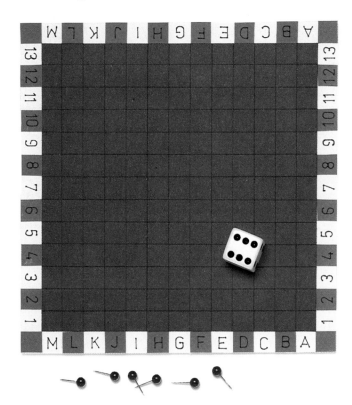

## ▲ Make the reference boards

Each player needs a reference board in order to keep track of which treasure chests he or she has looted. It is basically a smaller version of the main playing board grid, but without the island. Paint one reference board in each of the player colors: blue, green, red and yellow.

▶ You may want to decorate your treasure island with a few shady palm trees. Cut out two identical tree shapes. Slit one from top to middle and cut the other from middle to bottom. Then slot them together so that they will stand up, as shown on page 11.

## ▼ Make the treasure chests

Cut out the shape below from stiff colored paper. Make line *x* the same width as a grid square, so that each chest fits exactly into one square. Fold along the solid pencil lines and glue the tabs as shown. Make six chests.

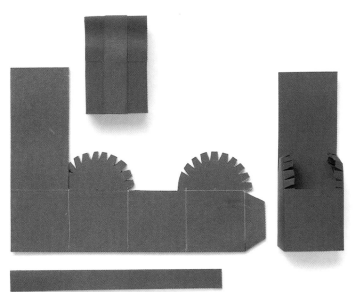

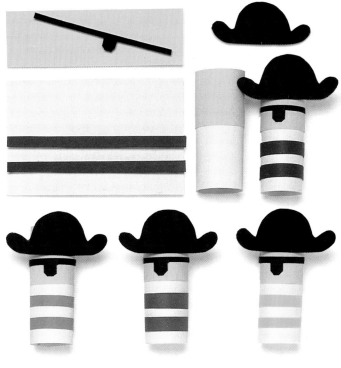

## ▲ Make the pirates

These are the playing pieces. Each pirate is a tube made from paper with a stuck-on face, eye patch, hat and stripes in each player's colors. Make two pirates for each player.

## ▼ Make the treasure cards

Make six of each card shown below. They should be slightly smaller than a grid square so that they fit neatly inside the pirates' chests.

## ▼ Make the ships

Cut the shape shown below from stiff paper. (The hole in the deck should fit a pirate.) Fold and glue the tabs. Make a ship for each pirate, with a flag in his or her player's colors.

## Playing the game

Play the treasure island game and collect as much buried treasure as you can!

**1** Shuffle the treasure cards and put six inside each chest. Put the chests on the island.

**2** Each player has one small board, two ships and two pirates. Players roll the die in turns to move their ships and pirates. You may split a die roll between pieces.

**3** Starting from your colored corner, move the two ships in opposite directions around the edge of the board.

**4** When your ships have reached the right coordinates for a treasure chest, the pirates jump out and move toward that chest in straight lines. You must throw an exact number for the pirates to land on the squares by the chest.

**5** When both pirates are in position, open the chest and take the top card. If you pick up a skull and crossbones, miss a turn and go back to the beginning.

**6** If you pick a treasure card, the pirates can return to their ships and then the ships can move on to the next set of coordinates.

**7** The game ends when one player has looted treasure from every single chest. The winner is the player with the most treasure.

◀ Use the small boards and map pins to record which treasure chests you have visited.

## Piracy!

Pirates often raid other ships. If you throw the exact number, you may move one of your pirates into an empty, unguarded ship. The ship's owner must then hand over one piece of treasure!

To read a map, you have to understand map "language" – all the different signs and symbols that maps contain. Some symbols are easy to make sense of. A cross, for instance, usually stands for a church. But you may need to look at the map **key** to work out the meanings of other, more complicated symbols.

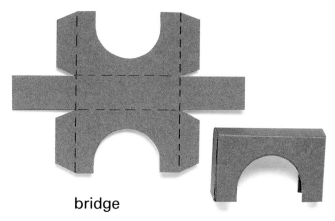

bridge

**1** Decide which features you would like to show on your map, and work out some simple shapes to represent them.

railroad station

factory

### MAKE it WORK!

Make a three-dimensional map with colorful models that stand up on a flat map base. Make your 3-D models out of poster board or modeling clay. Then follow the instructions on pages 16–17 to draw the map base. You could plot out a sketch map of your own neighborhood or design an imaginary town plan.

### For the map symbols, you will need

colored poster board   X-Acto knife
scissors                modeling clay
glue                    toothpicks

**2** Many 3-D models can be based on a box shape, with four sides and a top. One of the simplest symbols is the bridge. Just cut out the shape shown at the top of this page, fold along the dotted lines and glue the tabs.

**3** Once you have perfected the bridge, you can experiment with the basic box shape. Try making more complicated buildings such as houses, the railroad station or the factory.

There are many ways to make 3-D map models. How about clay models or flat cardboard shapes attached to toothpicks?

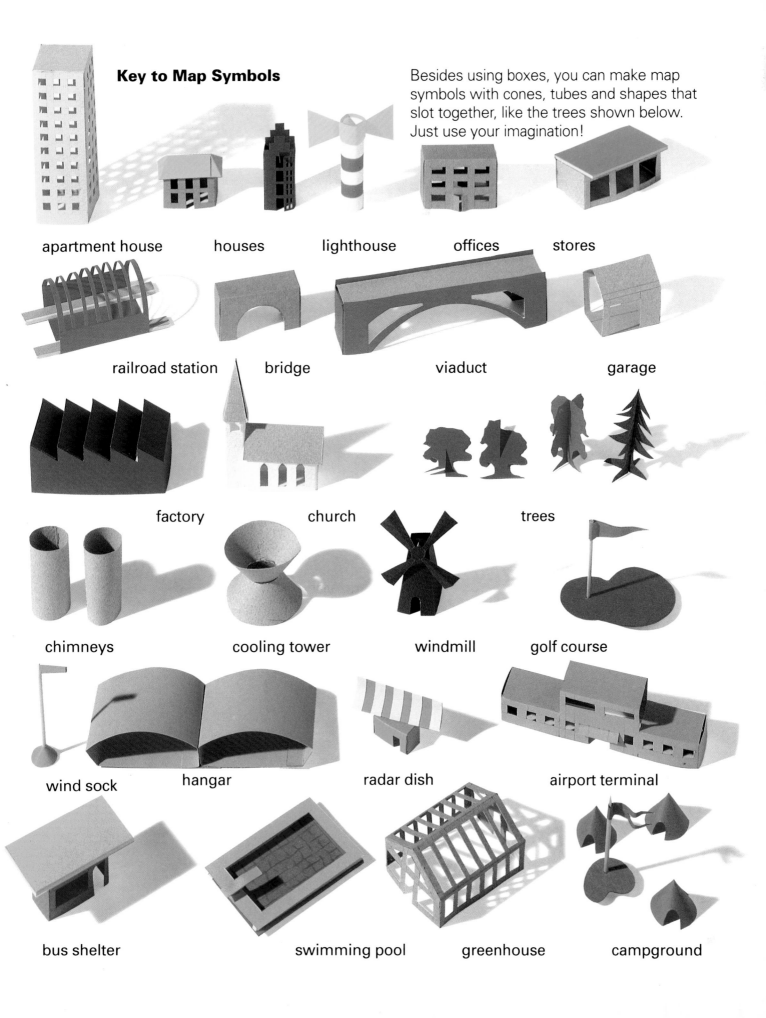

**Key to Map Symbols**

Besides using boxes, you can make map symbols with cones, tubes and shapes that slot together, like the trees shown below. Just use your imagination!

apartment house

houses

lighthouse

offices

stores

railroad station

bridge

viaduct

garage

factory

church

trees

chimneys

cooling tower

windmill

golf course

wind sock

hangar

radar dish

airport terminal

bus shelter

swimming pool

greenhouse

campground

## Making the map base

When you have made some map models, you are ready to plot out the map base.

## For the map base you will need

| | |
|---|---|
| a compass | thick poster board |
| graph paper | pens and pencils |

**1** Start outside your house by placing the compass flat on the ground. The needle will point north.

**2** Twist the compass around so that the compass marker for north is in line with the needle. Draw an arrow pointing north at the top of your sheet of paper.

**3** Now draw in your street at the correct angle in relation to north.

**4** Walk along the street and draw in the other streets and roads. As you go along, make notes of any buildings or features that might need special map symbols. **Be careful** if the road is busy. Watch out for traffic.

**5** When your sketch is finished, draw a neater, larger version of the same map on a sheet of poster board and color it in.

**6** To make your map more authentic, you can draw thin grid lines across the base and mark coordinates around the edges.

**7** To finish off the map, add the 3-D models that you have made. You can also make a key to help other people read the map.

▼ You don't have to stop with a map of your neighborhood. You can also make up a map to show an imaginary town or village.

# 18 Scale and Contours

The shape of the land is usually shown on maps using contour lines. These lines join up all the points that have the same height. They are drawn at regular intervals – every 50 to 100 yards, for instance. Steep hills and mountainsides appear on maps as a lot of contour lines drawn close together.

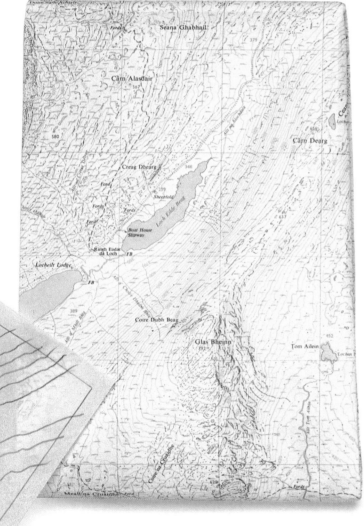

## You will need

| | |
|---|---|
| a relief map | X-Acto knife |
| tracing paper | glue |
| pens and pencils | paint |
| thick cardboard (from an old cardboard box) | |

## Scale

Most maps are drawn to a scale. The distances and shapes on the map stand for real distances and shapes on the ground – but everything on the map is much smaller. A map might have a scale of one mile to one inch, for example. One mile on the ground would then be shown as one inch on the map.

## MAKE it WORK!

Turn the contour lines on a flat map into a 3-D cardboard model and then experiment with the scale of your model.

**1** Take a section of a map with contour lines showing a hilly or mountainous area. Trace the contours onto a piece of tracing paper. If there are very many contour lines close together, you can make the transfer of contour lines more simple by only drawing every second or third line.

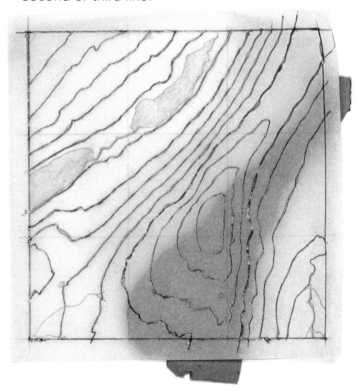

**2** Turn the tracing paper onto its back and go over the lines with a thick pencil, pressing down hard. Then turn the tracing paper right side up again and lay it on top of the piece of thick cardboard.

## Scaling up

See for yourself how scale works by increasing the scale of your model to make it twice as big.

**1** Choose a small section of your map to double in scale and copy the contour lines onto a piece of tracing paper.

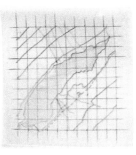 

**2** Draw a grid of squares sized one inch by one inch onto the tracing paper, as shown above.

**3** On a second piece of tracing paper, make up a larger grid of squares, two inches by two inches. Then draw the contour lines onto this larger grid, copying their exact shapes but making them twice as large. If you copy the lines square by square, you'll find it's quite easy.

**4** Trace the larger grid contours onto a piece of thick cardboard. Build up the model as you did before but, this time, glue down a double layer of cardboard for each contour line. That way, you'll be making the scaled-up model twice as high as the original one, as well as twice as big on the ground.

**3** Copy the shape of the lowest contour onto the cardboard by going over the lines once more with a pencil.

**4** Ask an adult to help you cut out the contour shapes with a sharp X-Acto knife.

**5** Now trace and cut each of the other contour shapes in turn.

**6** Cut a large piece of cardboard to be the base of the model.

**7** Now glue the contour shapes into position. Begin by putting down the shape of the lowest contour. Then add the other contours one by one, in order of height.

**8** When you have glued all the cardboard shapes in place, you could add other details to your model, such as streams and lakes.

**Be careful** as you use the X-Acto knife. Hold the cardboard firmly and always cut away from you.

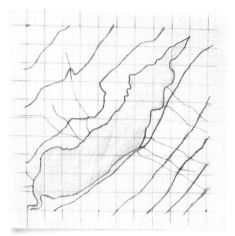

# 20 Mapping Mountains

Mountains are measured up from the level of the ocean, which is the same all over the world. The peak of Mount Everest, the world's highest mountain, is 29,028 feet above sea level.

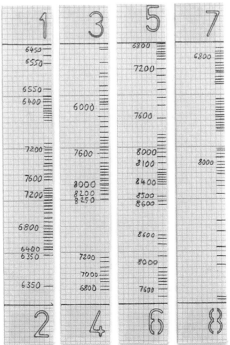

*Maps are plotted by surveyors. To work out the height of the land, they use an instrument called a **theodolite** (or transit). It measures distances and the angles made by imaginary lines between points on the ground. From these measurements, surveyors can calculate heights above sea level.*

## MAKE it WORK!
You can make a stand-up model of a mountain by reading and understanding the contour lines on a flat map.

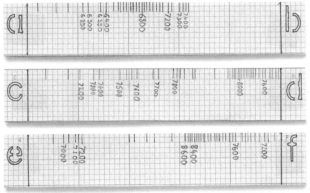

## You will need
a large-scale contour map of a mountain
graph paper       thin poster board
X-Acto knife      wooden skewer

**1** Find a contour map that shows a large hill or mountain. We have chosen to make a 3-D model of Mount Everest.

**2** Draw a large grid onto the contour map. Number and letter the grid lines as shown.

**3** Cut a strip of graph paper for each grid line. Put letters and numbers on the strips to match the grid lines.

**4** Take each strip of graph paper in turn and mark off the contours that cross that grid line. Write the height of the contour beside each mark. If your map shows steep slopes mark only every fifth or tenth contour.

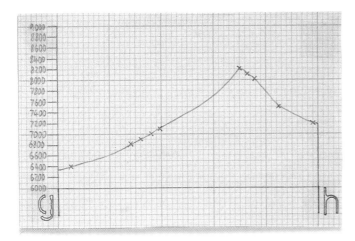

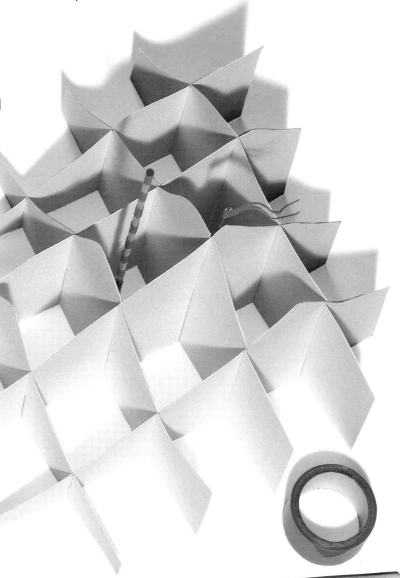

◀ Contour measurements plotted onto a graph sheet

▶ Cutout cross section of graph paper

You can make your mountain look even more realistic by pasting a thin layer of papier-mâché over the poster board framework. Once the papier-mâché is dry, paint the mountain, using green for the grassy, lower slopes and black and brown for the steep, rocky areas.

**5** For every strip, make a graph sheet like the one above. Write the same scale of heights on the left side of every sheet, with the lowest contour measurement at the bottom and the highest at the top.

**6** Transfer the contour line readings from the strips onto the graph sheets. Join up each of the points measured and cut out the shapes.

**7** Draw around these shapes on poster board and then cut them out again to make cardboard cross sections of the mountain.

**8** Cut slits in all the lettered cross sections from the bottom of the poster board up to the middle. Cut slits in all the numbered sections from the top down to the middle.

**9** Now slot the lettered sections into the numbered sections, putting them all in the right order. Your mountain will take shape like the one in the picture.

**10** Make a measuring pole from a wooden skewer or thin dowel. Draw in the height markers, using the same scale as that on the graph sheets.

Planet Earth is shaped like a ball, about 8,100 miles across. Inside the earth, there are a series of different layers of hot rocks and metals.

The earth's outer layer is called the crust. Most scientists believe that this is made up of about twenty huge rafts, or plates, that fit together just like the pieces of a giant jigsaw. The study of these **continental plates** is known as the science of **plate tectonics.**

*How do scientists know about the earth's different layers? The deepest hole that has ever been drilled is only 6 miles deep, so it does not even go all the way through the earth's outer crust. However, scientists have discovered ways of studying the shock waves sent out by earthquakes. These waves travel at different speeds through different kinds of material, and they can tell us a great deal about the rocks and metals inside the earth.*

## MAKE it WORK!

A good way to see the earth's layers is to make a clay model planet for yourself. You will need blue, yellow and green clay for the land and oceans on the crust, and five other colors for the five layers inside.

**1** Start with the inner core, the very center of the earth. Scientists believe that it is made of solid iron and nickel at a temperature many times hotter than boiling water. The inner core is about 1,600 miles in diameter.

**2** Now add the outer core. It is made out of hot, liquid metals, and is estimated to be 1,400 miles thick.

**3** Next wrap the lower **mantle** around the core. It is 1,250 miles thick.

**4** The upper mantle is 450 miles thick. It contains both solid rocks that have melted and then cooled down again, as well as hot, liquid rock called **magma**.

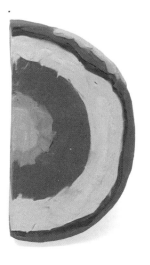

**5** Now add a thin layer of Plasticine to be the earth's rocky crust, which is only 20 miles thick. Then mold on the earth's surface features – the oceans and continents.

**6** When your clay ball is complete, cut out a wedge shape to show a cross section of the earth's different layers.

## MAKE it WORK!

Volcanoes form along cracks in the earth's crust, usually where two continental plates meet. Hot, liquid rock, gas and steam come welling up through the crust from the layer underneath. You can make your own spectacular model volcano and cause an eruption of bubbly gas using vinegar and baking soda.

molding the
modeling clay

cross section of
volcano

### You will need

vinegar
red food coloring
baking soda
a plastic beaker

a large cardboard box
modeling clay
damp sand

**1** Color the vinegar with red food coloring.

**2** Put the baking soda into a narrow beaker. It should be about half full.

**5** Cut the cardboard box in half and place the clay shape inside it. Then pile up sand in the box and mold it into your volcano shape. Make sure that you leave the top of the volcano and all the side tunnels clear.

**3** Make a long cardboard funnel and fit it neatly around the beaker.

**4** Cut three or four holes in the side of the funnel. Then mold the clay around it. Leave the top open and make tunnels in the clay, leading down to the holes in the side of the funnel.

**6** When it is time for an eruption, pour the red vinegar into the beaker and stand back! **Be careful** when you try this project, as it can be very messy! It's probably best to wear old clothes and stage the eruption outside!

We don't usually notice it, but the surface of the earth is moving all the time. The continental plates that fit together to form the earth's crust shift a small amount every year, less than an inch at most. Yet the effects of these tiny plate movements can be enormous. Where plates bump into one another, violent earthquakes may happen, and the pushing and pulling of plates over millions of years has created many of the earth's mountain ranges.

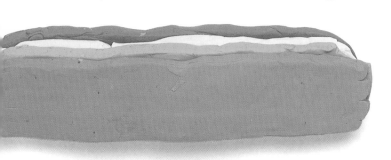

## MAKE it WORK!

The movement of the earth's tectonic plates has caused two main types of mountain range. In **fold mountains**, the crust of the earth has wrinkled up into wavy folds. In **fault-block mountains**, the pressure of the moving plates has cracked brittle layers of rock, shifting and tilting blocks of the earth's crust.

Make some simple models of faulting and folding, using strips of modeling clay.

## You will need

modeling clay          a modeling clay cutter

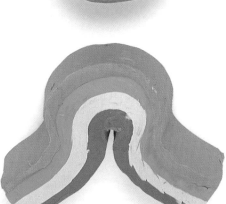

*The bottom of a fold in the Earth's crust is called a **syncline**.*

*The top of a fold is called an **anticline**.*

**1** Take four or five strips of clay and lay them on top of one another, as though they were layers of rock in the earth's crust.

**2** Hold the clay at both ends and push it together. It will bend into the shape of a fold mountain – either a syncline or an anticline.

**3** Now take another strip of clay and slice through it once or twice with the clay cutter. Slide the pieces of clay against one another as though the rock were pushing up or down.

*When faulting pushes a section of the earth's crust upward, the raised rock is called a **horst**. When the faulting thrusts a section of crust downward, it makes a **graben**.*

## Make a tectonic jigsaw

Make a world map jigsaw and see for yourself how the earth's continental plates fit together.

## You will need

a world map          thick cardboard
tracing paper        a sharp X-Acto knife
pens and pencils     paint and glue

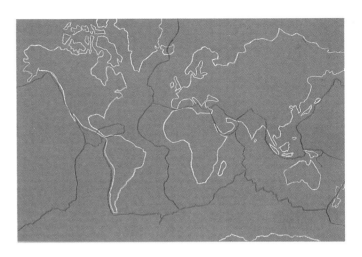

**1** Copy a map of the world onto tracing paper with a red pen. Then turn the paper over and rub the pencil hard across the back of the red line.

**2** Turn the tracing paper back onto the right side and place it on the piece of thick cardboard. (The side of an old cardboard box will do fine.)

**3** Draw over the outline of the world map again, pressing down firmly as you do so. The pencil on the back of the tracing paper will transfer onto the cardboard.

**4** Ask an adult to help you cut around the land shapes with a sharp X-Acto knife. **Be careful!** Cut away from you and hold the cardboard firmly.

**5** Take another large piece of thick cardboard and glue the pieces of land into position on it. If you wish, you can then paint the seas and oceans in blue.

**6** Now copy the shapes of the continental plates onto your map. Follow the sketch map above or look in an atlas for a more detailed map of the continental plates.

**7** Cut along the breaks in the continental plates to make your jigsaw pieces.

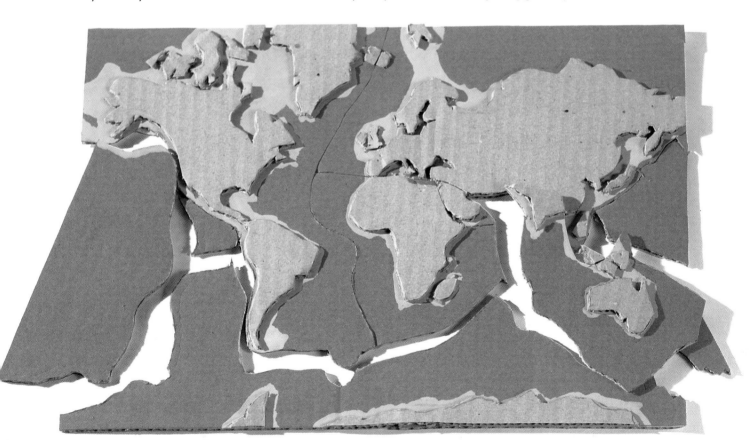

Rocks are solid lumps of **minerals** that make up the Earth's crust. There are basically three different ways in which rocks are created – so rocks are usually classified by geologists in these three different categories:

● **Sedimentary** rocks. They are made of layers of sand and silt that have been squashed together.

● **Igneous** rocks. They are rocks that became so hot that they melted but then cooled down again and solidified.

● **Metamorphic** rocks. These are sedimentary or igneous rocks that have been altered by the action of heat or pressure.

## MAKE it WORK!
Make a collection of rocks, label them and classify them. Geologists study rocks carefully, examining their texture and the way they have been formed.

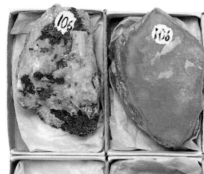

105 granite

106 chrysocolla

17 realgar

15 copper ore in sandstone

63 magnetite

**1** Collect some samples of the rocks in your local area. This might be quite difficult if you live in a town, so you can add to your collection with common rocks such as coal. You could also search for rocks if you visit the country or the seaside. It's even possible to buy unusual rocks at a special rock and gem store.

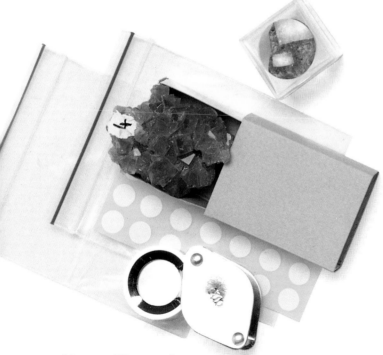

### You will need
a geologist's hammer
a magnifying glass
plastic bags
used matchboxes
glue

tissue paper
correction fluid
a notebook and pen
a reference book on
    rocks and minerals

**2** Make some specimen holders for your collection of rocks. Collect the trays from used matchboxes and stick them together to make larger trays with six or nine compartments. Inside each compartment put a layer of tissue paper for the rock to rest on.

38 rose quartz

14 quartz

27 sadallite

19 jet

10 limestone

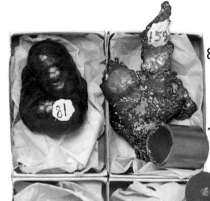

81 iron ore

159 copper ore

3 calcite

37 diamond

8 topaz

4 iron pyrites (fool's gold)

**3** Number the rocks. Dab white correction fluid in one corner and write the number in ink.

**4** Make a fact sheet for each rock. Draw the rock and record where it came from. If you don't already know exactly what it is, find out by looking for it in a reference book.

▼ Some rocks contain fossils, the imprints of prehistoric plants and animals. The dying plant or animal fell to the ground and was covered over by mud or soft earth. As the earth slowly hardened into rock, the plant or animal's imprint remained, in vivid detail.

## Hard and soft rocks

One way of classifying rocks is according to how hard they are. A scale of hardness for minerals was worked out by the Austrian scientist Friedrich Mohs in 1812. The scale goes from one to ten, and a rock in one band of the scale can scratch only the rocks below it. At the top of the scale, at number ten, is the diamond, which can scratch anything. At the bottom is talc, a rock so soft that you are most likely to have seen it ground up as a powder and used to keep babies' bottoms dry!

▼ Mohs based his hardness scale on the ten types of rock shown below.

### ▶ Making limestone

Limestone contains the mineral **calcite**. It occurs in many different forms and is often shaped by the action of water.

The most spectacular limestone formations are the giant pillars that grow in limestone caves. As water passes through a cave, it dissolves calcite from the surrounding rocks. Then, as the water drips and dries, it leaves behind little deposits of calcite that gradually build up into **stalactites** and **stalagmites**.

## You will need

| | |
|---|---|
| two tumblers | string |
| distilled water | saucer |
| soda crystals | paper clips |

**1** Half fill both tumblers with distilled water. Then gradually pour in as many soda crystals as the water can dissolve. This mixture is called a **saturated solution** of soda.

**2** Dip a length of string into the solution. Then run it from one tumbler to the other, with the saucer in between. Fix it in place with paper clips as shown, and wait for three or four days.

1 talc

2 gypsum

3 calcite

4 fluorite

5 apatite

6 orthoclase

7 quartz

8 topaz

9 corundum

10 diamond

*Stalactites with a **c** grow from the ceiling.
Stalagmites with a **g** grow from
the **ground**.*

**3** The solution travels along the string as if it were the roof of a cave. When it reaches the lowest point, the solution then drips into the saucer. Water dries in the air, leaving soda deposits to form a hanging soda stalactite. A soda stalagmite will also grow upward from where the solution drips onto the saucer.

### ▶ Growing crystals

A crystal is a piece of matter whose **atoms** join together in a regular shape. Rock crystals form when a saturated solution of certain kinds of mineral slowly **evaporates**. If the crystal then comes back into contact with the same saturated solution, it may continue to grow.

### You will need

| | |
|---|---|
| a tumbler | a saucer |
| distilled water | a length of cotton |
| copper sulphate powder | a pencil |

**1** Make up a saturated solution of warmed distilled water and the copper sulphate powder. Tip a little bit out onto a saucer.

**2** The water will slowly evaporate and leave behind some copper sulphate crystals. Choose the largest of them and tie a piece of cotton around it. Then suspend it from a pencil into a tumbler of solution as shown.

**3** Now be patient! Over the next three to four weeks, your crystal will slowly get bigger.

**Be careful** when you use copper sulphate powder! It is poisonous.

Soil is made from rocks and minerals that have been ground up and mixed with water, air and the remains of dead plants and animals. Like rocks, soils have different characteristics. Some are better for growing crops than are others.

## MAKE it WORK!

Soil settles in different layers, or **strata**. The largest, heaviest particles are usually those at the bottom (the **subsoil**), with the finest particles in the **topsoil** nearest the surface. Make your own cross section of soil layers in an old plastic bottle.

**1** Using a funnel made from folded poster board, half fill the bottle with soil and top it up with water.

**2** Put the top on the bottle and shake it well for a couple of minutes. Then let it stand. After several hours, the soils will have settled to the bottom of the bottle.

**3** Now siphon off the water, taking great care not to disturb the settled soil. Put one end of the plastic tube into the bottle. Suck a little on the other end, but as soon as the water starts to move along the tube, quickly take it out of your mouth. Once it gets going, the water will keep flowing into a container placed beneath

### The colors of soil

Mix soil from different strata with a little water and smear the paste onto white poster board. Now you will be able to see the variety of soil colors.

### You will need

a plastic bottle
a mixture of soils,
   dug out of one hole
   in the earth at
   different depths
poster board

water
plastic tubing
a knitting needle
a sharp X-Acto knife
cardboard

**4** To drain off any last drops of water, make some small holes with a knitting needle in the bottom of the soil bottle and leave it for a few minutes in a sink or basin.

**5** Ask an adult to cut off the top half of the bottle and then lay it on its side. Carefully slit it lengthwise in two. Slide a piece of cardboard down the slit as you cut, so that you don't let any soil fall out. Now you can inspect all the different layers.

## Testing soil

Soils may contain chemicals that are either **acids** or **alkalis**. Scientists measure these chemical properties on something called a pH scale. Acid chemicals have a pH rating between 0 and 7. Alkalis come between 7 and 14 on the scale. Scientists and farmers often test the pH value of soils – acid soil is less likely than alkaline soil to be rich in the minerals that crops need to grow.

▲ Acids turn purple litmus paper pink.

▼ Alkalis turn pink litmus paper purple.

## MAKE it WORK!

Perform your own soil test. The easiest way is to use litmus paper. It is treated with a special dye, which reacts to acids and alkalis by changing color.

## You will need

tumblers                distilled water
soil samples            litmus paper strips

**1** Put a soil sample in a glass tumbler. Add distilled water to it.

**2** Mix the soil and water well. Then leave the glass to stand for a few minutes.

**3** Dip a pink litmus strip into the water above the soil and see what happens. If the soil is acid, the color will not change. If your soil is alkaline, the pink paper will turn purple.

**4** Now dip a purple litmus strip into the water and see what happens. If your soil is acid, the purple strip will turn pink. If it's alkaline, the color will not change.

**5** If neither the pink nor the purple litmus paper changes color much, you should classify your soil as neutral—it is neither very acid nor very alkaline.

The earth is surrounded by a layer of gases called the **atmosphere**, or air. Unless there's a strong wind, we don't usually notice the air and tend to think that it has no weight. But, in fact, air is always pressing up, down and sideways, and air pressure is a strong force.

Changes in the air pressure are connected to the earth's weather conditions. As a general rule, falling air pressure means that wet or stormy weather is on the way. High pressure usually brings fine, sunny weather.

**1** Cut the neck off the balloon and stretch the top over the glass jar. Fix it firmly under the rim of the jar with a rubber band so that the jar will be airtight.

**2** Fix the jar to the wooden base with strong glue or a blob of adhesive gum.

**3** Cut a point on one end of the straw. Glue the other end to the balloon rubber, which you stretched across the top of the jar. Use a very tiny dab of rubber cement.

**4** Cut off a long strip of poster board, fold it three times and glue it together to make a stand-up triangle. Then fix the triangle to the wooden base of the barometer.

## MAKE it WORK!
Meteorologists measure the air pressure using an instrument called a **barometer**. It usually contains mercury, a heavy, liquid metal that is very sensitive to changes in both pressure and temperature. These mercury barometers give very accurate readings, but you can also make a much simpler barometer for yourself, using little more than a balloon and a glass jar.

## You will need
a glass jam jar
a balloon
rubber bands
a piece of wood
rubber cement

adhesive gum
a thick plastic straw
colored poster board
a spirit level
graph paper

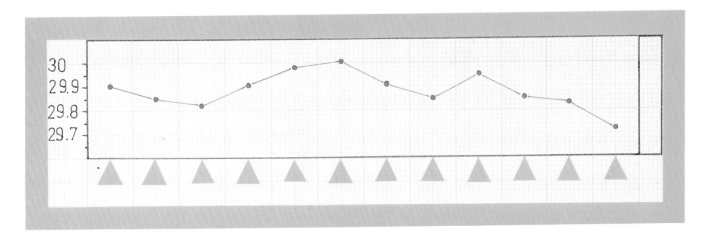

**5** Use the spirit level to hold the straw just level and mark a line on the card. This will be the midline. Rising pressure is recorded above that line, falling pressure below it.

### How the balloon barometer works
When air pressure increases outside the glass, it pushes down on the balloon, making the point of the straw go up. When air pressure falls, the air inside the jar expands and pushes the balloon up, so that the straw dips down.

### ▲ Keeping a record
This graph shows changes in air pressure. The readings were taken in Chicago over a period of twelve days during October. Which days do you think were most likely to be fine and sunny? When might it have rained?

Plot the readings from your own balloon barometer onto a line graph.

*Air pressure is much stronger at ground level than high up in the earth's atmosphere. Less pressure makes the air thinner, so that people cannot breathe properly.*

Have you ever been out on a blustery day and wondered what causes wind? It is the air around the earth, which is always on the move. Warm air is lighter than cold air. As it heats up, the warm air rises, making an area of low pressure and allowing colder, heavier air to rush in and fill the space.

### Kites

Kites are a good way of observing the wind. You can feel how strong it is and watch the direction in which it is blowing. In the nineteenth century, before airplanes were invented, meteorologists often used kites to record temperatures and measure wind speeds high up in the sky.

### MAKE it WORK!

Make your own box kite and take it outside to test the breeze.

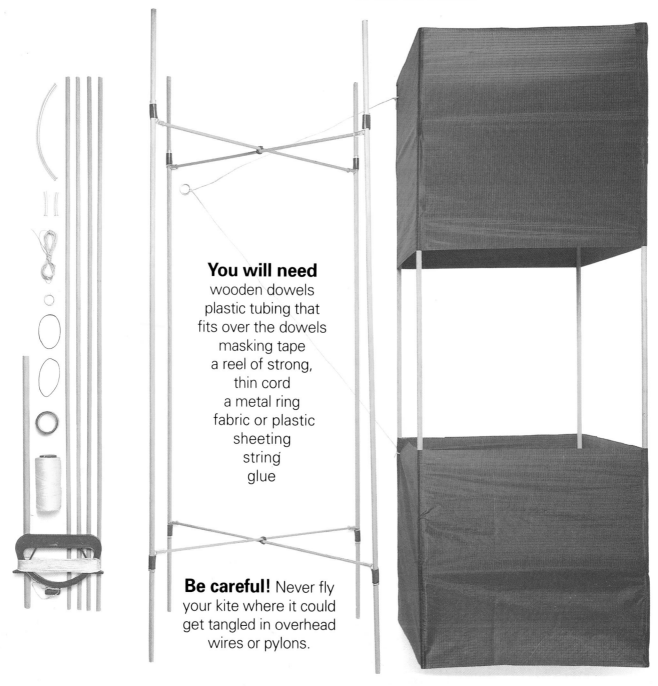

**You will need**
wooden dowels
plastic tubing that
fits over the dowels
masking tape
a reel of strong,
thin cord
a metal ring
fabric or plastic
sheeting
string
glue

**Be careful!** Never fly your kite where it could get tangled in overhead wires or pylons.

**1** Ask an adult to cut the doweling into four long sections and four shorter crosspieces.

**2** Cut the plastic tubing into eight sections. Slice halfway through each piece of plastic to make the joints where the cross sections meet the uprights. Follow the diagram below.

**3** Tape the joints into position and reinforce them with extra masking tape, if necessary. Secure the cross sections in the middle with rubber bands or string.

**4** Measure out two pieces of fabric or plastic sheeting to fit around the top and bottom thirds of the kite frame. Glue them onto the struts, leaving the middle section free.

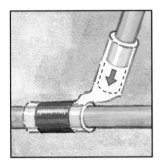

**Making the joints**

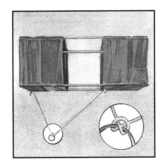

**Attaching the bridle**

**5** Now make the kite's bridle. Cut a piece of string that is slightly longer than the kite itself. Tie the metal ring onto this string, two-thirds of the way along.

**6** Then fix the short end of string to the top of one strut, with the long end tied onto the same strut, two-thirds of the way down. Getting the angle of the bridle correct is important for an easy lift-off.

**7** Tie one end of the reel of strong cord onto the metal ring. Wind the rest around a piece of thick dowel (or you could buy a special plastic kite handle from a kite shop). Now you are ready to fly your kite.

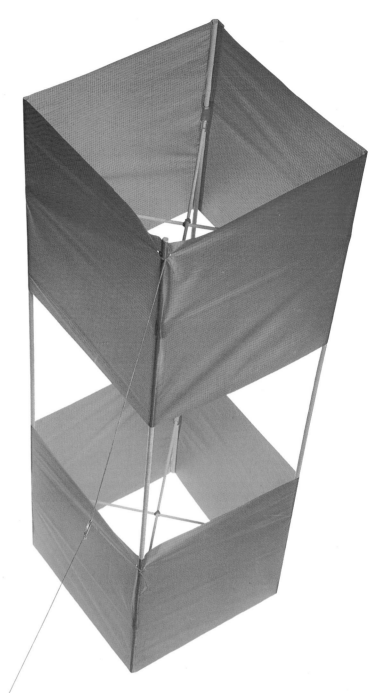

*Kites have a long history and were probably first invented by the Chinese about 3,000 years ago. Besides being helpful to weather forecasters, kites have also been used in research by many other scientists. In 1752, Benjamin Franklin built a homemade kite to conduct the famous experiment that proved that lightning is a form of electricity. The brothers Orville and Wilbur Wright also experimented with box kites when they were developing the world's first airplane in 1903.*

# 36 Wind Speed

Winds vary from gentle breezes to sudden, violent storms that may cause destruction and death. Some of the strongest winds are hurricanes. They form over the oceans in tropical regions when air is sucked into an area of low pressure. Storm clouds often whirl around the center, or eye, of the hurricane faster than a high-speed train.

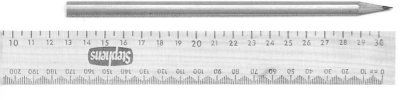

## MAKE it WORK!

You may never see hurricane-force winds, but every place has calm days and windy days. Make an **anemometer** – a simple wind gauge – and record daily wind speeds in your area.

**1** Take a piece of thick wooden dowel that fits neatly into the copper pipe. This will be the anemometer's upright.

**2** Ask an adult to help you drill a hole through the upright. The hole should have the same diameter as one of the thin dowels. Cut a slit in either end of this thin dowel. Thread it through the upright, gluing it in place as shown.

**3** Cut an arrow head and an arrow flight out of poster board and fix them to the ends of the thin dowel.

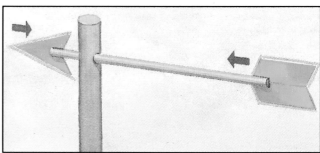

**4** Cut a quarter circle out of colored poster board and tape it onto the arrow.

**5** Take the bottom from a plastic half-gallon soda bottle and cut slits in the sides so you can attach it to the flat wooden stick.

**6** Ask an adult to drill a small hole in the other end of the flat stick and then pin or nail it to the top of the upright, making sure that it can move about freely.

**7** Choose a spot outside. Hammer the copper pipe into the ground and then put in the upright. Hold it in position with a map pin. Check that the upright is vertical by hanging a washer on a string from the wind arrow. The string should hang absolutely straight.

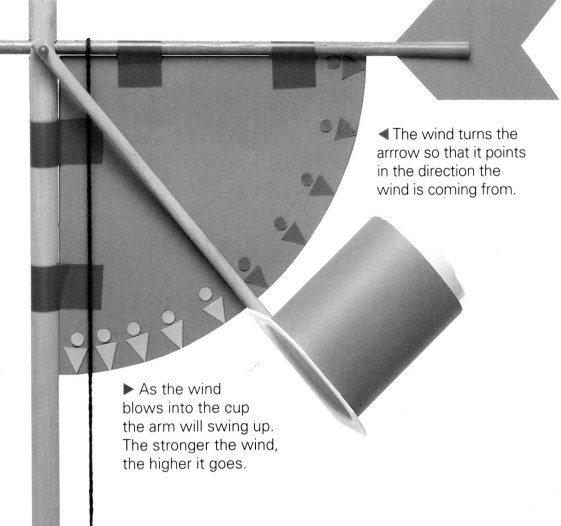

## You will need

thick wooden dowel
a copper pipe
thin wooden dowels
glue
colored poster board
waterproof tape
a plastic cup
map pins
string and a washer

▼ Wind speeds are shown on weather maps by the number of flights on the symbol for wind.

**Force 2**

**Force 3**

**Force 4**

**Force 5**

**Force 6**

**Force 7**

**Force 8**

**Force 9**

**Force 10**

**Force 11**

**Force 12**

◀ The wind turns the arrrow so that it points in the direction the wind is coming from.

▶ As the wind blows into the cup the arm will swing up. The stronger the wind, the higher it goes.

## The Beaufort Scale

This is a scale for measuring wind speed, based on observing nature. It was invented by a British admiral named Sir Francis Beaufort, well over two hundred years ago.

| | |
|---|---|
| **Force 1** | Calm. Trees are still. |
| **Force 2** | Slight breeze. Leaves rustle. |
| **Force 3** | Light breeze. Leaves move all the time. |
| **Force 4** | Moderate breeze. Branches move. |
| **Force 5** | Fresh breeze. Small trees sway. |
| **Force 6** | Strong breeze. Large branches sway. |
| **Force 7** | Near gale. Whole trees sway. |
| **Force 8** | Gale. Branches blown down. |
| **Force 9** | Strong gale. Slight damage to buildings. |
| **Force 10** | Storm. Widespread damage. |
| **Force 12** | Hurricane. Total destruction. |

# 38 Wind Direction

Wind direction varies according to the changing seasons and shifting patterns of low and high pressure. Winds are described by the direction from which they are blowing. Westerly winds come from the west, for example.

Wind direction has a strong influence on the weather. In Europe and North America, for instance, northerly winds usually mean cold weather. In the same way, if a wind is blowing across a stretch of ocean, it is more likely to bring rain than if it comes from across a desert or over a mountain range.

## MAKE it WORK!

A simple weather vane shows where the weather is coming from at any one particular time – but meteorologists also need to record wind direction over a longer period. Make your own wind recorder and use it to build up a picture of long-term wind patterns, so you don't have to run out and check a weather vane ten times a day.

**1** Glue an empty thread spool inside the bottom of a shoe box, slightly off center, as shown on the left. Fill the box with sand or small stones in order to weight it down.

**2** Make a hole in the top of the box, lined up with the spool below. Glue a second spool around the hole and then pass the dowel through the spools and hole.

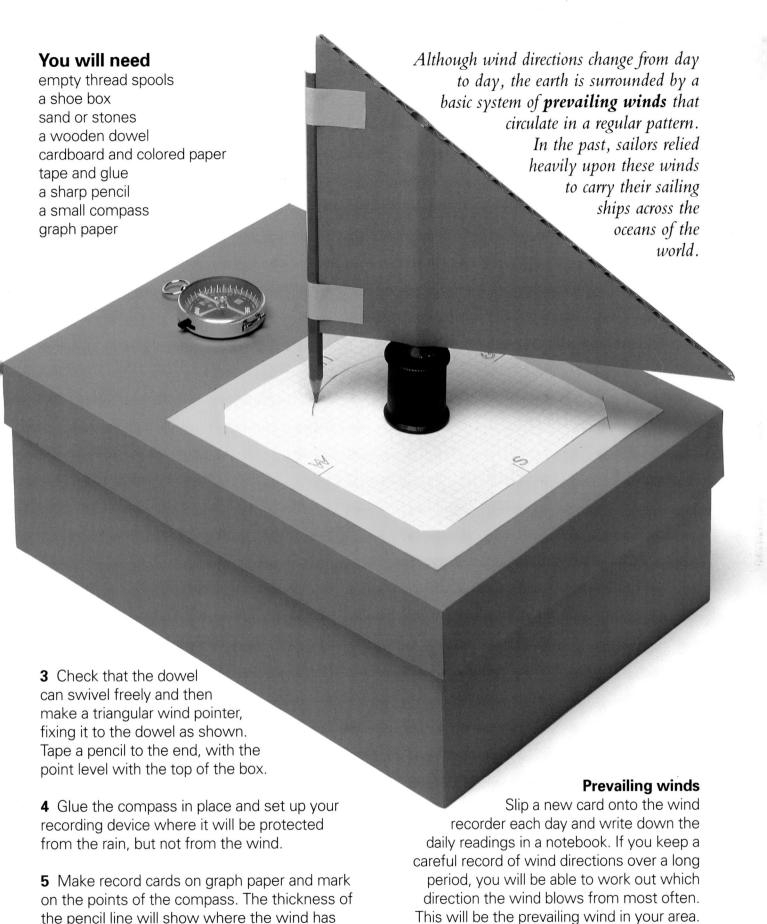

## You will need

empty thread spools
a shoe box
sand or stones
a wooden dowel
cardboard and colored paper
tape and glue
a sharp pencil
a small compass
graph paper

*Although wind directions change from day to day, the earth is surrounded by a basic system of **prevailing winds** that circulate in a regular pattern. In the past, sailors relied heavily upon these winds to carry their sailing ships across the oceans of the world.*

**3** Check that the dowel can swivel freely and then make a triangular wind pointer, fixing it to the dowel as shown. Tape a pencil to the end, with the point level with the top of the box.

**4** Glue the compass in place and set up your recording device where it will be protected from the rain, but not from the wind.

**5** Make record cards on graph paper and mark on the points of the compass. The thickness of the pencil line will show where the wind has been blowing from most.

### Prevailing winds

Slip a new card onto the wind recorder each day and write down the daily readings in a notebook. If you keep a careful record of wind directions over a long period, you will be able to work out which direction the wind blows from most often. This will be the prevailing wind in your area. Does it change from season to season?

Rain clouds are formed by the action of the sun on oceans, seas and lakes. When it is heated, the earth's surface water turns into **water vapor** and rises, like steam, into the warm air. This warm air continues to rise, but, as it cools down, the water vapor condenses into rain clouds. Eventually, the clouds become so thick and heavy that the rain falls back to earth.

## MAKE it WORK!

Keeping a record of rainfall is a very important part of a meteorologist's work. Farmers in particular need to know the pattern of rainfall so that they expect dry and wet weather at the right times. Make a simple rain gauge yourself and use it to measure the rainfall in the area near your home.

### ▼ Plastic bottle rain gauge

Cut off the top of a plastic bottle to make a funnel. Turn it upside down and push it into the body of the bottle, remembering to take the lid off first! Using a ruler, mark measurements on the bottle with waterproof tape.

▲ The simplest way of predicting the weather is to study the shapes and colors of different clouds. Puffy, white clouds, high up in the sky, usually mean fine weather. But low, gray clouds often bring rain. If you have a camera, you can experiment with taking some photographs of clouds. Keep a record of the day and weather conditions each time you take a photograph.

## You will need

half-gallon plastic
   soft drink bottle
scissors
a ruler
waterproof tape
a plastic funnel
a glass jar
graph paper

## Taking readings

Measure rainfall in your gauge just after it has
stopped raining or early every morning before
the sun evaporates any of the water in your jar.
To reduce evaporation, you can also keep the
gauge in a hole in the ground.

## ▶ Quick-acting rain gauge

You can make a quick-acting rain gauge using
a plastic funnel and a glass jar. Put the funnel
inside the jar, fixing it in place with waterproof
tape. The large area of the funnel will collect
more rain than a straight jar will.

   A quick-acting rain gauge is very handy for
comparing how much rain falls from day to day
in one place. But it doesn't give exact readings
of rainfall in inches – you should use a plastic
bottle rain gauge for that.

*Different parts of the world have different
amounts of rainfall. Deserts lie far from the
path of rain-bearing winds and may go for
years without rain. Other places have some
rain every day. However, in most regions
the rainfall varies from season to season.*

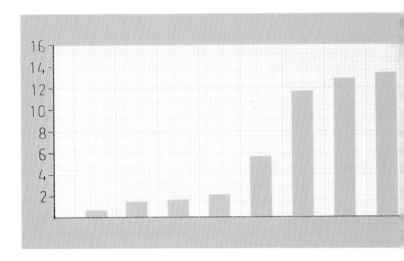

## ▲ Keeping records

Record the amount of rain that falls every day,
every week and every month. You can then
log the information on a bar chart.

# 42 Temperature

Measuring temperature changes is an important part of a meteorologist's work. Farmers need to know if falling temperatures are likely to cause a frost and damage their crops. Police want to warn motorists if there is ice on the roads. And everyone likes to know whether to dress warmly or put on light summer clothes.

### Thermometers

We measure temperature with an instrument called a thermometer. Many thermometers contain the liquid metal mercury, which is ideal for showing temperature changes. It has a very low freezing point, a very high boiling point, and expands at a regular rate as it gets warmer.

### MAKE it WORK!

Make your own thermometer using colored water, which also expands with heat. It will never be as accurate as mercury, but a water thermometer does give you a rough idea of changing temperatures.

**1** Ask an adult to drill a hole in the cork. It should be just wide enough for the plastic pipe to fit through snugly.

**2** Push the pipe through the cork so that it just sticks out a little at one end. (**Be careful** not to hurt yourself as you do this.) Use a blob of modeling clay to hold the plastic pipe in place. Then tape a long, thin measuring piece of cardboard behind it.

**3** Fill the bottle to the rim with water that has been dyed with food coloring.

## You will need

cork
thin clear plastic
  pipe
modelling clay
cardboard and tape
food coloring
a glass bottle
a glass jug
ice cubes
graph paper

*Temperature is measured in degrees—either degrees Fahrenheit (°F) or degrees Celsius (°C). Water freezes at 0 °C and boils at 100 °C.*

**4** Put the bottle in a jug filled with ice cubes. The water level should sink a little. (Water contracts as it cools to 4° C. Below this temperature, it starts to expand again.)

**5** Seal up the bottle with the cork. Make sure it fits very tightly so that the water now has nowhere to go except up the tube.

**6** When the water has contracted to its smallest volume, mark the place on the measuring cardboard. You will know that, at this point, the temperature is 4° C.

**7** Take your thermometer out of the ice. As it warms up, the water will rise in the tube.

**8** You can mark more temperatures on the measuring cardboard using a mercury thermometer as a guide. Or just mark on a high point and a low point and watch the temperature change.

▶ This is a greenhouse thermometer. It shows the temperature at the present time but also records the highest and lowest temperatures that it has reached. The thermometer in the picture gives the current temperature as 18° C but also shows that, since it was last reset, the temperature has fallen to 6° C and risen to 28° C.

▼ With a greenhouse thermometer, you can take a daily reading of maximum and minimum temperatures and plot them onto a line graph.

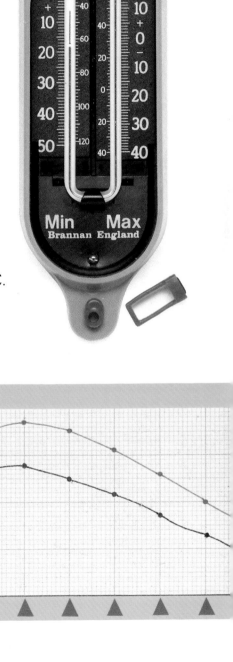

When scientists perform experiments, they always carefully control the conditions in which they work. You should control your experiments too.

Say, for example, that you want to record the temperature in your garden every day. You should always keep the thermometer in the same place. Otherwise, you won't be doing a fair test. Some parts of your garden may be more sheltered from the wind or have more direct sunlight than others. Moving the experiment around will then affect the results as much as real changes in temperature.

## MAKE it WORK!

Professional meteorologists and keen amateur weather forecasters keep some of their more sensitive instruments in a special shelter called a Stevenson screen. Changes of temperature and air pressure can be accurately recorded inside the screen – the air can get into the screen through the slats, but the instruments are protected from other forces such as strong winds and direct sunlight.

**1** Ask an adult to cut the plywood as shown. You will need a square for the bottom and a slightly larger square for the roof. Also cut two angled sidepieces to support the sloping roof, a wide strip to support the front of the roof and a narrow strip for the back. The angled sidepieces should be the height of the front section at one end and taper to the height of the back section at the other end.

### You will need
| | |
|---|---|
| plywood | metal chains |
| a jigsaw | wood |
| glue | paintbrushes |
| nails | wood primer |
| hinges and screws | undercoat |
| | white gloss paint |

**2** Now make four slatted screens. With an adult, cut eight sidepieces with angled notches in them for the slats to rest on. Your slats must face downward so start from the bottom, gluing and nailing each one in place.

**3** Glue a piece of wood across the top and bottom of each slatted screen as shown, and then screw them in place for extra strength.

**4** Now make the legs from four equal lengths of strong, square section wood. The shelter should stand about three feet off the ground.

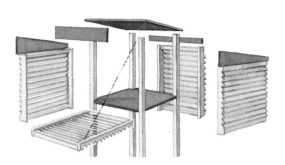

**5** Nail and glue the frame together as shown in the diagram, taking care to slope the roof away from the door so that rain can run off it.

**6** Three of the slatted screens are fixed firmly to the main frame. Put hinges and chains on the fourth screen to make a slatted door.

**7** To reflect the sunlight, the screen should be painted white. You will also make it weather-resistant by giving it three layers of paint – first a coat of wood primer, then an undercoat and finally a smart coat of white gloss.

**8** Position your screen out in the open, and you are ready to start making your weather records. You could also make a colorful weather vane, using dowels and balsa wood, and fix it onto your weather station.

**Acid** A type of chemical. Foods that contain acids, such as lemons, taste sour or sharp.

**Alkali** A type of chemical. In science, alkalis are the opposites of acids. One common kind of alkali is magnesia, the white powder we take to ease an upset stomach. Some vegetables, such as cabbages, grow well in alkaline soil.

**Anemometer** An instrument that measures the speed or strength of wind.

**Anticline** The top of a fold in the earth's crust.

**Atmosphere** The gases making up the air that surrounds the earth.

**Atoms** Tiny particles, over a million times smaller than the thickness of a human hair. Everything around us is made up of atoms – they are like building blocks, and by combining different atoms in various ways, different substances are created.

**Barometer** An instrument that is used to measure air pressure.

**Calcite** A mineral that is found in limestone. Calcite deposits form stalagmites and stalactites. Calcite is also used by industry as an ingredient in cement, paint and glass.

**Continental plates** The earth's crust is split into about twenty large sections, or plates. The shapes of the earth's continents reflect the shapes of the continental plates.

**Coordinates** On maps, coordinates are two sets of letters or numbers that refer to a particular point on the map's grid.

**Evaporate** When a liquid evaporates, it turns into a vapor, usually because it has been heated. When water evaporates, it becomes steam, or water vapor.

**Fault-block mountains** Mountains formed when sections of the earth's crust cracked and shifted up or down.

**Fold mountains** Mountains that have been formed when sections of the earth's crust have been pushed together and the surface has wrinkled into wavy folds.

**Geography** The study of the earth's surface. Physical geography examines the earth's natural features. Human geography is the study of how humans live on different parts of the earth.

**Geology** The study of the earth's structure, especially its rocks and minerals.

**Graben** A word used by geologists to describe a section of land that has shifted downward between two faults in the earth's crust.

**Horst** A piece of land that has been thrust up between two faults in the earth's crust.

**Key** On a map, the key explains the meaning of the special symbols.

**Magma** Hot, molten rock, which usually forms in the earth's upper mantle.

**Mantle** The upper layers of rocks and minerals beneath the earth's crust.

**Meteorology** The study of the weather.

**Minerals** Minerals are substances, such as rocks or metals, that are not living things. Anything on the earth that is not an animal or vegetable (or made from animal or vegetable products) is a mineral.

**Plate tectonics** The study of the earth's continental plates and their movements.

**Prevailing winds** A region's prevailing winds are those that blow most often from one particular direction.

**Saturated solution** Many substances, such as sugar or calcite, dissolve in water to make a mixture, or solution. However, water can absorb only so much of any given substance. When a measure of water has dissolved the maximum amount of a substance, the mixture is called a saturated solution.

**Stalactite** A long, thin finger of limestone that hangs from the roof of a cave or cavern.

**Stalagmite** A long, thin deposit of limestone that grows up from the floor of a cave.

**Strata** Layers, usually of rock or soil.

**Subsoil** The bottom layers of soil in the ground, nearest to the solid rock.

**Syncline** The bottom of a fold in the earth's crust.

**Theodolite** An instrument that is used for measuring the height of land.

**Topsoil** The layer of soil nearest the surface of the ground. It contains the finest soil particles.

**Water vapor** Tiny particles of water, suspended in the air. Steam is a form of water vapor.